KW-326-717

OXFORD Primary GEOGRAPHY

Series Consultant **3** **Steve Harrison**

Phil Almond Pam Jervis
John Lancaster Lynn Lancaster

OXFORD

The publishers would like to thank the following for permission to reproduce photographs:

AA Photo Library: 21 bottom; Mark Carney: 8, 10; Celtic Picture Library: 26 top & bottom; Glasgow City Council: 26, 27, 41 top left & bottom left; Robert Harding Picture Library: 46, 47 middle; The Hutchison Library: 47 top; David Hosking/Frank Lane Picture Library: 20 bottom; Walter Scott (Bradford) Ltd: 6; Scottish Youth Hostels Association: 41 right; The Telegraph Colour Library: 35; Wales Tourist Board:16 bottom, 17 left, 22 bottom, 24; John Noble/Wilderness Photo Library: 47 bottom.

All other photographs are by John Lancaster and Pam Jervis

The front cover picture was by John Walmsley Photo Library and Tony Stone Images.

Maps by Jeff Edwards. All other illustrations by Oxford Illustrators.

LIVERPOOL HOPE
UNIVERSITY COLLEGE

Order No. / Invoice No.

L097000031 Donation

Accession No.

281410

Class No.   Oxfl

372.91T   ALM

Control No.

1583

Catal.   12/12/97

Oxford University Press, Walton Street, Oxford OX2 6DP

Oxford   New York
Athens   Auckland   Bangkok   Bombay
Calcutta   Cape Town   Dar es Salaam   Delhi
Florence   Hong Kong   Istanbul   Karachi
Kuala Lumpur   Madras   Madrid   Melbourne
Mexico City   Nairobi   Paris   Singapore
Taipei   Tokyo   Toronto

and associated companies in
Berlin and Ibadan

All rights reserved. No part of this publication may be reproduced, stored in a retrieval system, or transmitted, in any form or by any means, without the prior permission in writing of Oxford University Press. Within the U.K., exceptions are allowed in respect of any fair dealing for the purpose of research or private study, or criticism or review, as permitted under the Copyright, Designs and Patents Act, 1988, or in the case of reprographic reproduction in accordance with the terms of licences issued by the Copyright Licensing Agency. Enquiries concerning reproduction outside those terms and in other countries should be sent to the Rights Department, Oxford University Press, at the address above.

Oxford is a trade mark of Oxford University Press

© Oxford University Press, 1996

ISBN 0 19 833472 9

Printed in Hong Kong

3 The caravan site in the photograph is in square 7219 (near Llanelltyd). Where else can tourists stay in this square?

4 What tourist features are found in grid squares:

a) 6915   b) 6618

c) 7318   d) 7217

5 You drive from Llanelltyd to Bontddu (G.R. 6718), then north to Llechfraith. How does the road change?

6 Photograph 2 shows the inn at Penmaenpool. What is its four figure grid reference?

7 Give the four figure grid references for

a) Dolgellau Hospital

b) Llyn Cynwch (a lake)

c) A farm trail

8 If you stayed at the inn at Penmaenpool, what activities could you plan for the week?

Barmouth

Barmouth is a small seaside town in North Wales.

The photograph shows Barmouth. It is built at the mouth of the Mawddach Estuary.

Tasks

Using the photograph

1 Describe Barmouth.

THINK about

Landscape

Leisure

Work

Size

Transport

Season

Shape

Using the photograph and map

The photograph shows part of the map.

2 Do you think the photograph was taken from Point A, B or C on the map?

3 In which direction was the camera pointing?

4 Name three features that photographs taken from the other points could have shown.

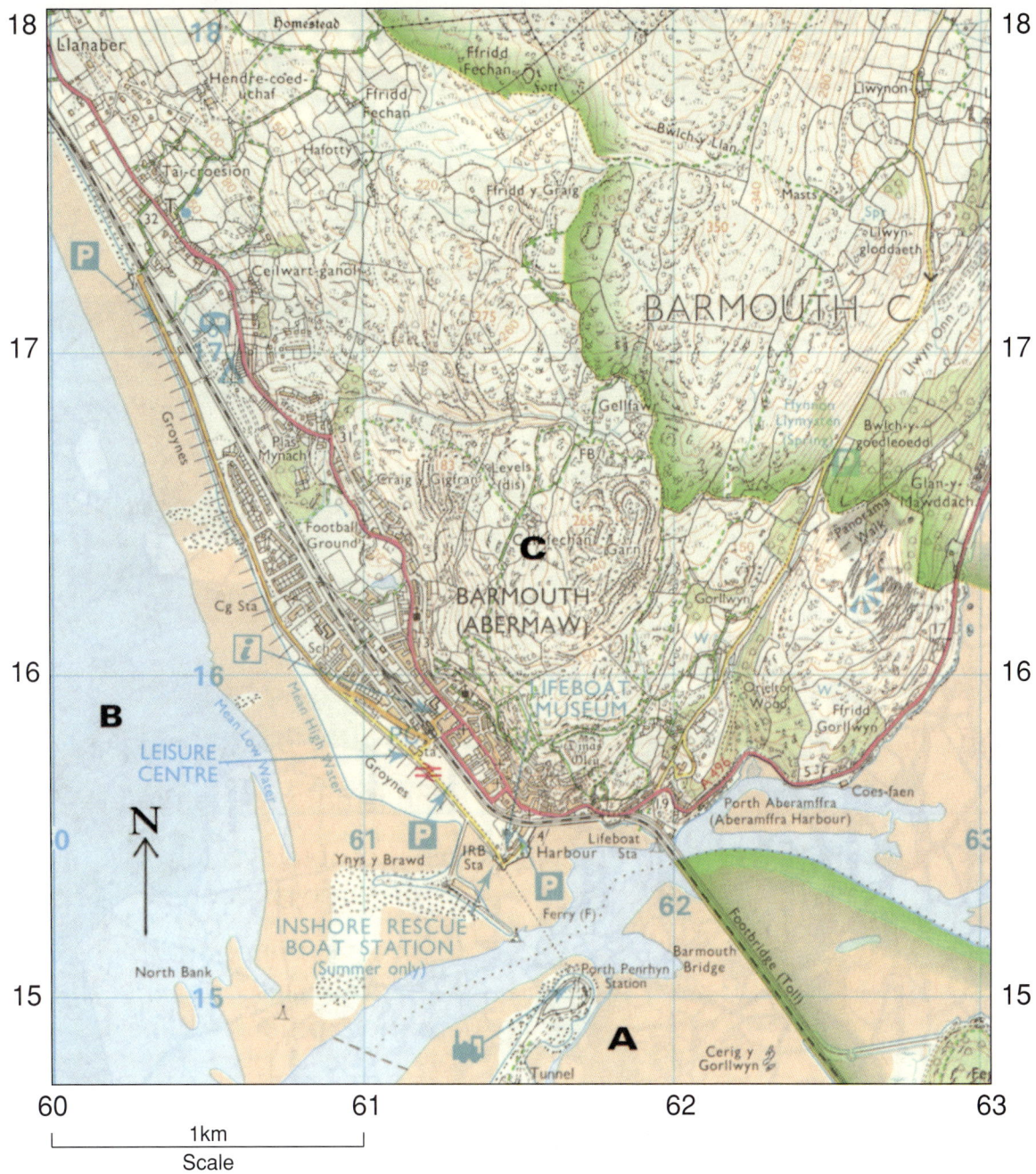

Scale

```
 |----1km----|
     Scale
```

Using the map

5 Give the four figure grid reference for:

   a) The railway station
   b) The football ground
   c) The lifeboat station
   d) The harbour
   e) A car park
   f) A panorama

6 How far is it from

   a) The harbour to the football ground?

   b) The caravan site to the lifeboat station?

7 Copy and complete the chart.

Feature	Location	Purpose
Groynes	Beach	Protect coastline
IRB Station		
Lifeboat Museum		
Barmouth Bridge		

25

BARMOUTH
A Seaside Locality

Until a hundred years ago, Barmouth was a small fishing port. Today it is a seaside resort. It is also a shopping centre for the local people. Most of the houses and shops are built out of local stone.

Tasks

1 Look at the photograph of St. John's Church. What do you think the roof and the walls are made from? Where do these materials come from?

2 What is the beach being used for?

3 Who might use the funfair?

4 What problems might the funfair cause for local people?

5 Look at all the photographs of Barmouth. Describe what the land around Barmouth is like.

26

Some of the houses have been made into hotels and restaurants. This is a photograph of a hotel.

6 What time of year was this photograph taken? How do you know?

7 What do you think happens to the people who work in the hotels at this time of year?

Look at the map of Barmouth.

8 Make two lists:

List A – Indoor activities.

List B – Outdoor activities.

9 Which five activities would be most popular with tourists?

To Panorama, famous for beautiful scenery

Mynach Road

Llanaber Rd.

To Llanaber and Harlech

Kings Crescent

Gellfachen Road

Panorama Road

To Dolgellau

Porkington Terr.

21 Mountains, walks and climbs

14

Pedestrian Level Crossing

13

18

11

10

25

Heol Y Lan

Park Road

King Edward St.

22

17

12

24

High Street

23

Old Town

Barmouth Bridge

19

Marine Road

15

Beach Rd.

20

9

Church Street

5

Promenade and Roadway

Marine Parade

16

Jubilee Road

6

7

Cardigan Bay

Sandy Beach

1

P

P

The Quay

Boating, fishing, sea and river trips

8 Ferry

1 Sandy beach	11 St. Tudwal's church	21 Mountain walks
2 Public gardens	12 Post office	22 Railway track
3 Footpath to Arthog	13 Park, tennis, bowls, & putting	23 Doctor's surgery
4 Lifeboat house	14 Children's playground	24 Police & council offices
5 St. David's church	15 Railway station	**Information centre**
6 Ty Gwyn	16 Bus depot	25 RAOB club
7 Ty Crwn	17 Footbridge	P Parking
8 Ferry to Fairbourne	18 Football ground	T Toilets
9 Old town	19 Coast guard lookout	Road unsuitable for vehicles
10 St. John's church	20 Theatre & community centre	

Origins and changes

Activities in settlements change over time.

Barmouth developed as a small fishing town and port in the 16th century. At first the main goods shipped were woollen clothes to London and Liverpool.

By the 18th and 19th centuries the most important cargoes were timber and railway sleepers. Oak was also used locally to build ships.

Tasks

1 Why do you think wool was shipped and not sent by road or rail in the 16th century?

2 What were railway sleepers made of in the 19th century?

3 What is the harbour used for today?

4 Do you think wool and timber are still important products in the port?

The railway opened in 1866. In the late 19th century Barmouth became a holiday town. In the past, local people visited Barmouth to shop and to go to chapel. Today some of the chapels have changed use.

Tasks

5 Why did the opening of the railway affect Barmouth as a holiday town?

6 Look at the photograph. What has happened to the chapel?

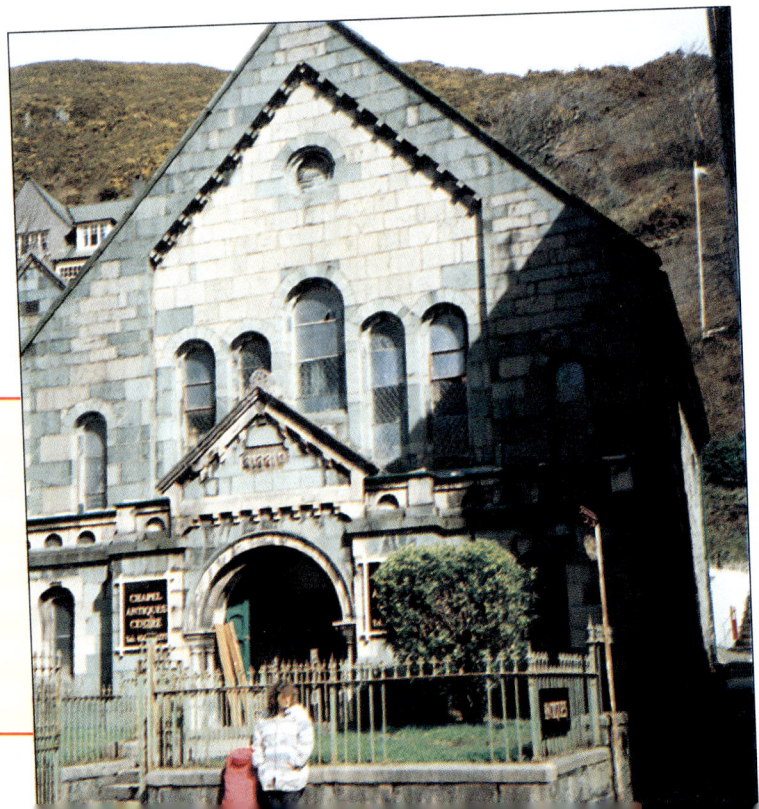

These photographs show Barmouth High Street in 1908 and today.

The High Street today

Barmouth, High Street, 1908

The High Street in 1908

7 Look at the buildings in both photographs. Using a table like the one below, make a list of what has changed and what has stayed the same.

Feature	Changed	Same
Chimneys		
Windows		
Roofs		
Walls		
Use		

8 Choose two things that have changed and describe what has happened.

9 Look at the street itself. Write a sentence about each of these features. Describe how the High Street has changed.

a) Road surface

b) Traffic

c) Street lighting

d) People

10 The width of the High Street is unchanged. What problems would that cause for today's visitors?

29

LIVERPOOL HOPE UNIVERSITY COLLEGE

Visiting Barmouth

BARMOUTH
A Seaside Locality

Symbols

✈ Airport or Airfield

🏛 Building of historic association or architectural interest

🏰 Castle or defensive works

✝ Cathedral, abbey, priory or notable Christian site

🎪 Country Park

🗼 Early Christian monument

🌳 Walk: Nature Trails, Forest Trails, Long distance walks, Town Trails, and Heritage Trails, Gardens

⚲ Prehistoric site of importance

🏛 Roman site

🎣 Sea Fishing boats

🏄 Surfing beach

ℹ️ Tourist Information Centre (see list on back of map)

🤿 Underwater swimming facilities

🎿 Water Skiing

⛵ Yacht or boat club

Tasks

Look at the tourist information map.

1 Make a list of five tourist attractions within 25 kilometres of Barmouth.

2 What time of year do you think most people would visit Barmouth. Why?

3 If you were visiting Barmouth, list eight attractions starting with your favourite.

4 Make a list of three attractions for someone over 65 years old. Explain your answer.

30

Children from a local school asked ten visitors about their visit to Barmouth using this questionnaire. The table below shows the results of their survey.

Visitors Survey
Date
Time
Where do you live?
How did you travel here?
How long did it take?
Why have you come?
Comments

Questionnaire Results Date: 14 May At Main Street				
Where live	Transport to Barmouth	Time taken	Reason	Comments about place
1 Bala	Bus	1 Hour	Visit friends	Quiet
2 Aberystwyth	Train	$\frac{1}{2}$ Hour	Shopping	Convenient
3 Liverpool	Car	3 Hours	Holiday	Nice town
4 Birmingham	Car	3 Hours	Holiday	Loves it
5 London	Car	6 Hours	Holiday	Nice place
6 Newcastle	Car	8 Hours	Holiday	OK
7 Manchester	Train	6 Hours	Holiday	Likes it
8 Wrexham	Bus	2 Hours	Holiday	No sun!
9 Bristol	Train	6 Hours	Holiday	Nice in summer
10 Cardiff	Car	4 Hours	Business	Likes it

Tasks

5 In which season were the questions asked?

6 How do you know?

7 How many visitors came from Wales? (Use an Atlas to help you with this one).

8 How many visitors were not happy with Barmouth? Why?

9 Which visitors travelled the furthest?

10 Draw a bar chart to show how the visitors travelled to Barmouth.

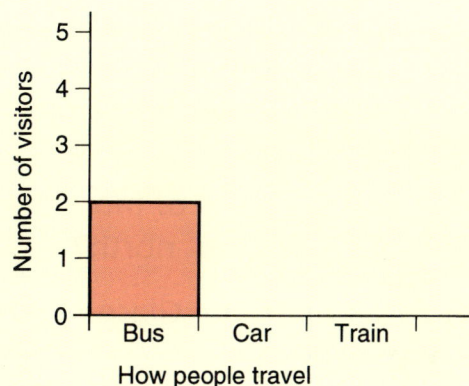

Number of visitors

5
4
3
2
1
0

Bus   Car   Train

How people travel

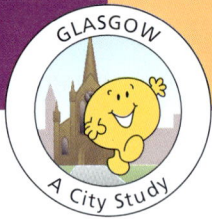

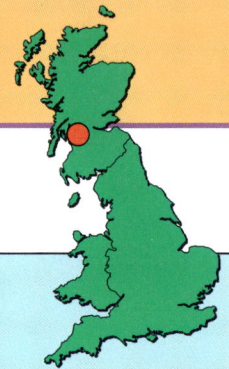

Glasgow is Scotland's largest city

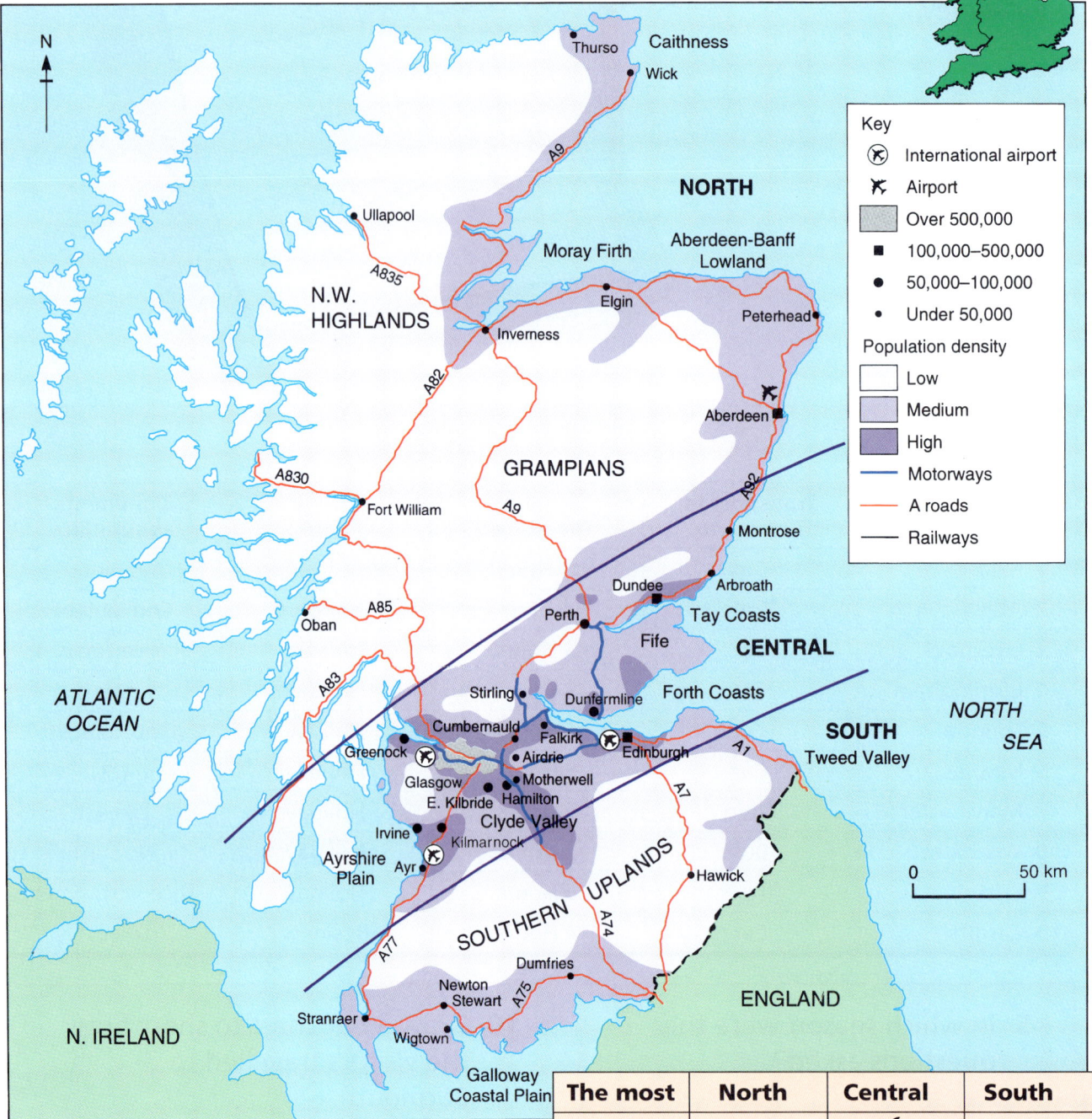

Map of Scotland showing population density, roads, railways, airports and regions.

Labels on map:

N

Thurso • Caithness
Wick •

NORTH

Ullapool •

Moray Firth   Aberdeen-Banff Lowland

N.W. HIGHLANDS

Elgin •
Inverness •   Peterhead •

Key
- (✈ circled) International airport
- (✈) Airport
- (shaded) Over 500,000
- (■) 100,000–500,000
- (●) 50,000–100,000
- (•) Under 50,000

Population density
- Low
- Medium
- High
- Motorways
- A roads
- Railways

GRAMPIANS

Aberdeen

A82
A830
Fort William
A85
Oban
A83

A9   A92

Montrose •
Dundee   Arbroath •
Perth   Tay Coasts
Fife   CENTRAL

ATLANTIC OCEAN

Stirling •   Dunfermline   Forth Coasts
Cumbernauld   Falkirk   Edinburgh   SOUTH   NORTH SEA
Greenock •   Airdrie •   A1   Tweed Valley
Glasgow   Motherwell •
E. Kilbride   Hamilton
Irvine   Clyde Valley
Ayrshire Plain   Kilmarnock   A7
Ayr   Hawick •

N. IRELAND

SOUTHERN   UPLANDS

A77   A74
Dumfries •
Newton Stewart   A75
Stranraer •   ENGLAND
Wigtown •
Galloway Coastal Plain

0   50 km

The most	North	Central	South
people		✓	
motorways			
railways			
airports			

Tasks

1 Which is the largest settlement in Scotland?

2 Which settlement of more than 100,000 is furthest north?

3 How far apart are Glasgow and Edinburgh?

4 The map of Scotland has been divided into THREE sections – North, Central and South. Copy and complete the chart above.

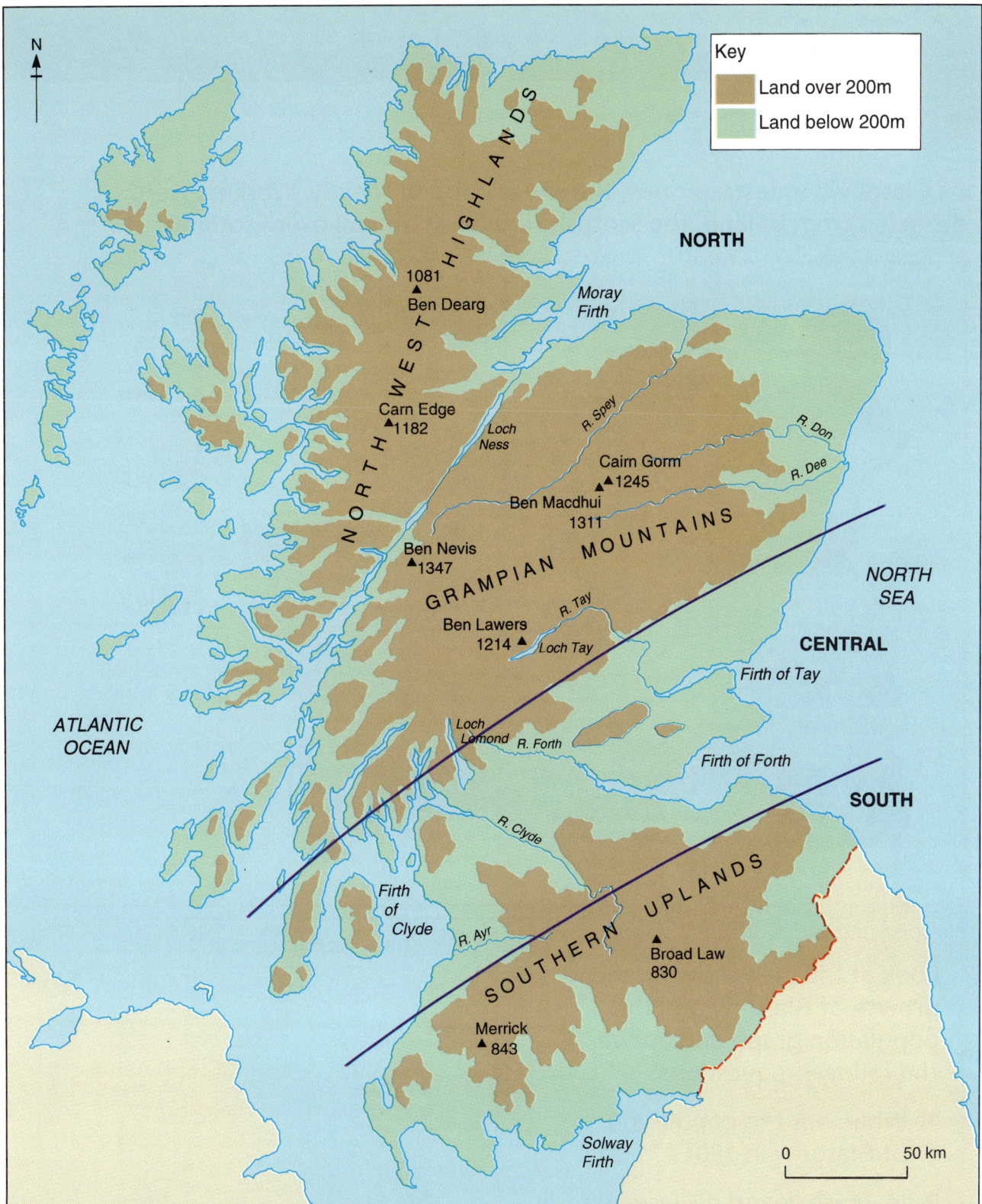

N

Key
Land over 200m
Land below 200m

NORTH WEST HIGHLANDS

1081 ▲ Ben Dearg

Moray Firth

NORTH

Carn Edge ▲ 1182

Loch Ness

R. Spey

R. Don

Cairn Gorm ▲ 1245

R. Dee

Ben Macdhui 1311

Ben Nevis ▲ 1347

GRAMPIAN MOUNTAINS

NORTH SEA

Ben Lawers 1214 ▲

R. Tay

Loch Tay

CENTRAL

Firth of Tay

ATLANTIC OCEAN

Loch Lomond

R. Forth

Firth of Forth

SOUTH

R. Clyde

Firth of Clyde

SOUTHERN UPLANDS

R. Ayr

Broad Law 830

Merrick ▲ 843

Solway Firth

0   50 km

5 Name three mountain ranges in Scotland.

6 Name four rivers which enter the North Sea.

7 Name two rivers that enter the sea west of Scotland.

8 Which is Scotland's highest mountain?

9 Are Scotland's major cities built on high land or low land?

10 Do most main roads run along the high land or low land? Why?

Tasks

33

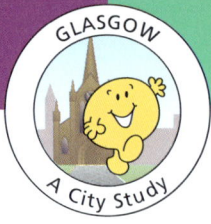

Glasgow: past and present

As Glasgow's industries grew, the city expanded rapidly. Workers were attracted from Ireland, the Scottish Highlands and all over Scotland.

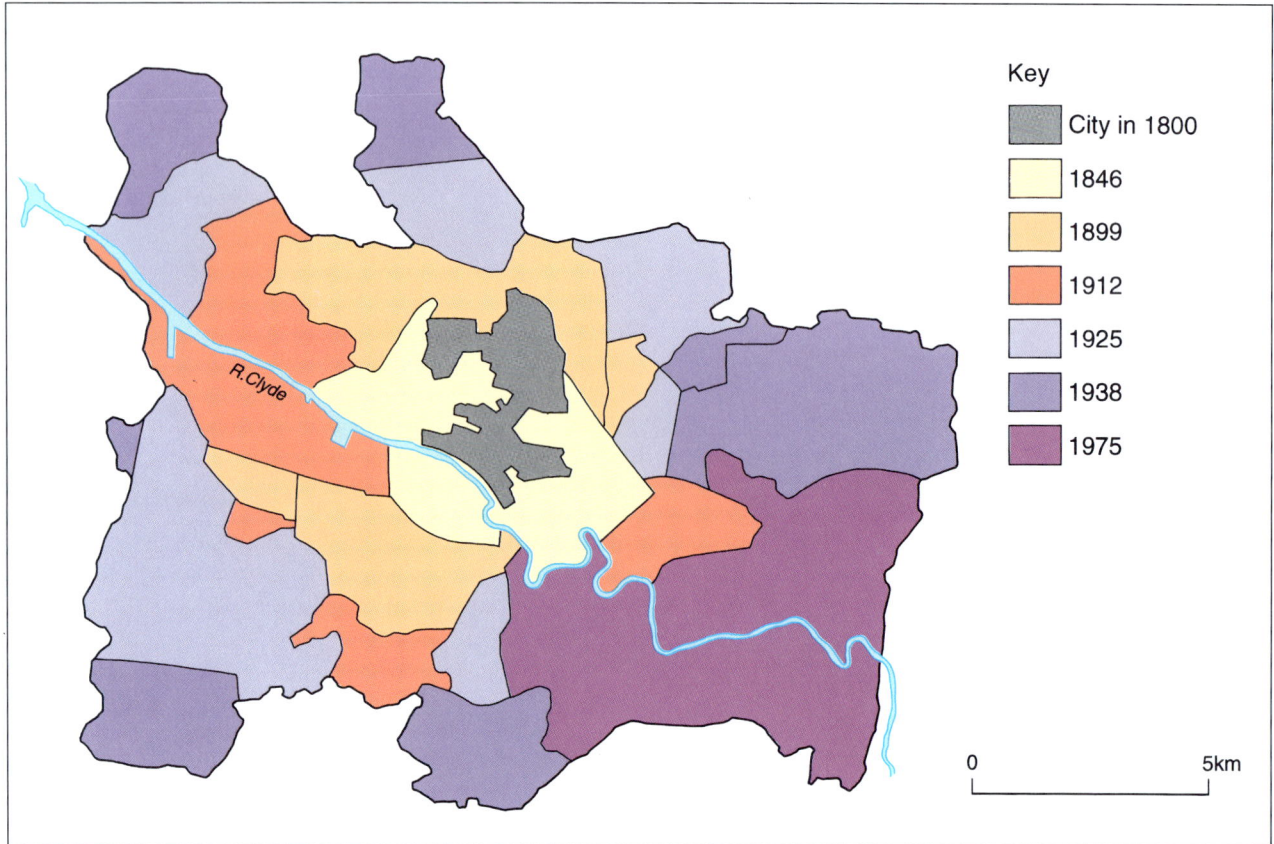

Key

	City in 1800
	1846
	1899
	1912
	1925
	1938
	1975

R.Clyde

0   5km

Tasks

Look at the map showing the growth of Glasgow and the population graph and answer the following questions:

Glasgow Population 1801–1995

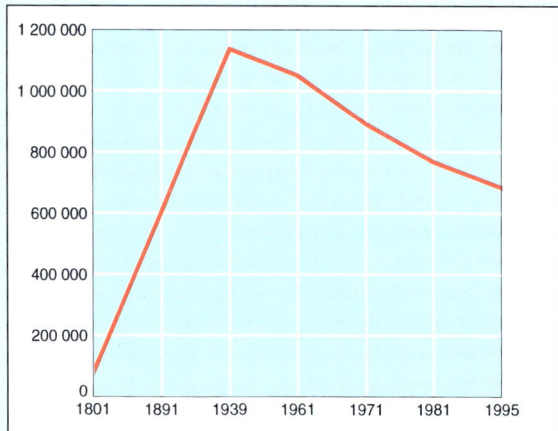

1 200 000
1 000 000
800 000
600 000
400 000
200 000
0
1801   1891   1939   1961   1971   1981   1995

1 What was the population of Glasgow in 1801?

2 In which year did Glasgow's population reach its highest? How many people were there?

3 At that time was the city larger or smaller than at present?

4 In 1800 on which side of the River Clyde was the city?

5 When did the city spread across the River Clyde?

6 Which part of the city was the last to expand?

Towns and cities have grown in size. Often settlements join together to form one large built up area called a conurbation. In doing so there is no farmland or open space left between settlements.

Scale 1 : 400 000
0   10 km

Tasks

Look at the map above showing the conurbation of Glasgow and answer the following questions:

7 Measure the conurbation from east to west. How far is it?

8 Which is the most northerly town in the conurbation?

9 List three settlements which were once outside the conurbation.

10 How do you think that the shape of Glasgow will change? Trace an outline of the conurbation and include other settlements that may be joined up. Describe its shape. Measure how large it is.

An aerial view of Glasgow.

35

Glasgow: image of the city

Most large cities try to attract new industry. This helps with jobs for local people as older industries are closing.

Glasgow had a drab old-fashioned image.

The city had to show the rest of the world that these images were not true of modern Glasgow if it was to attract firms and visitors.

> It's a dangerous place.

> It's full of vandals.

> There are no jobs there.

> It's a dirty old industrial town.

Spiers Wharf (before)

Spiers Wharf (after)

Tasks

Look at the two photographs of Spiers Wharf on the Forth and Clyde Canal.

1 What do you think that these buildings were used for in the past?

2 Describe the changes that have taken place in the two pictures. In what ways are the buildings the same/different?

3 What do you think that the buildings are used for today?

4 What sort of image did Glasgow have in the past? Why do you think this came about?

5 What kind of image is given by the pictures on this page?

6 How has the area around the Cathedral been improved? What would you add?

Glasgow Garden Festival '88

GLASGOW'S MILES BETTER

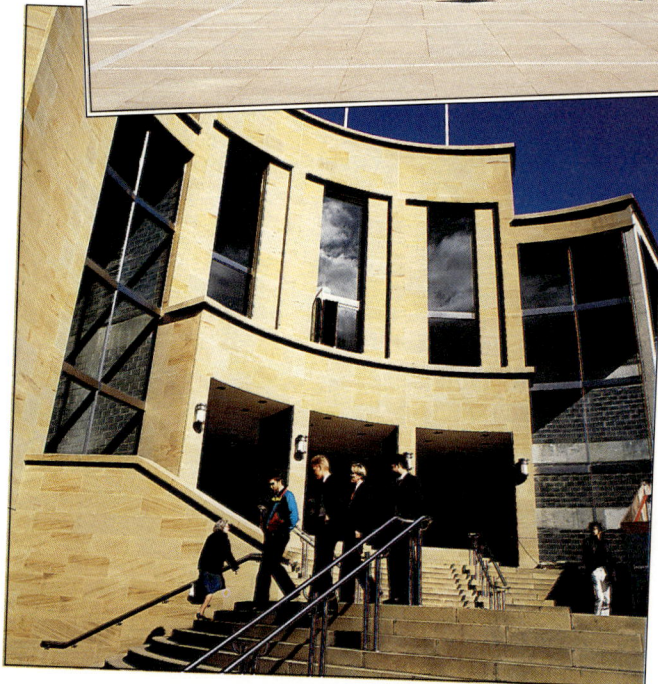

THINK about

traffic

protection of plant life

materials used

lighting

pedestrians

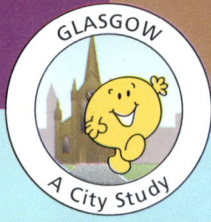

British visitors to Glasgow

How and why do visitors travel to Glasgow?

Key — Visitors from

Key	Visitors from
34%	Scotland
2%	Wales
4%	N. Ireland

English regions

%	Region
5%	North
7%	Yorkshire
12%	North west
7%	Midlands
24%	South east
5%	South west

— Motorways
— A roads
— Railways

ATLANTIC

OCEAN

Orkney Is.
Stromness
Scrabster
Thurso
A892
Wick
A9
Isle of Lewis
Stornoway
Harris
Tarbert
The Minch
A835
Ullapool
N. Uist
Lochmaddy
Uig
A87
A82
Kyle of Lochalsh
Inverness
A96
A9
S. Uist
Lochboisdale
Isle of Skye
Barra
Mallaig
Aberdeen
Coll
Tiree
A82
A9
A94
Colonsay
A85
Oban
A84
A9
Dundee
Islay
M80
M73
Glasgow
M8
M9
Kintyre
Bute
M8
M8
Edinburgh
Arran
Ardrossan
A74
A1
M74
A7
Cairnryan
A75
A74
Coleraine
A2
Londonderry
A6
M22 M2
Larne
A5
M1
Belfast
A1
Newry
A2
Cairnryan
Stranraer
Workington
A66
Newcastle upon Tyne
A69
Sunderland
A1(M)
Tees/Hartlepool
Middlesbrough
A66
A19
Scarborough
North Channel
Isle of Man
Douglas
Sligo
N16
N15
N4
Castlebar
N17
Longford
Drogheda
N5
N1
Galway
N6
N4
Dublin
Dun Laoghaire
Holyhead
A5
A55
Heysham
Leeds
York
A64
A1
Fleetwood
M55
Bradford
Blackpool
M6
M61
Manchester
M62
Kingston upon Hull
A15
Immingham/Grimsby
Liverpool
M58
M57
Chester
Sheffield
M1
Crewe
Stoke-on-Trent
A50
Nottingham
Shrewsbury
M54
A38
A1
King's Lynn
Norwich
Birmingham
M6
Leicester
Great Yarmouth
A49
M42
Coventry
A11
A12
Cambridge A45
Ipswich
Felixstowe
M1
Luton
Harwich
A40
Oxford
M40
M11
A1(M)
M25
London
Southend-on-Sea
Fishguard
A40
Newport
M4
Swansea
Cardiff
M4
M32
Bristol
M5
Medway
Sheerness
Ramsgate
M3
M25
M26 M20 M2
Dover
Bristol Channel
A303
A3(M)
A23
Folkestone
A259
A30
A35
Brighton
Newhaven
Exeter
A30
Southampton
M27
Portsmouth
A38
Weymouth
Poole
Isle of Wight
Torquay
A30
Plymouth
Penzance

Irish Sea
St. George's Channel
N3
N7
N9
N11
Limerick
Shannon Estuary
N18
N20
N21
Tralee
N22
N25
Cork Harbour
Cork
Waterford
Wexford
Rosslare
Milford Haven
Pembroke

0   50   100 km

English Channel

1 From which country do most British visitors come to Glasgow?

2 From which English region do the most come?

3 From which region would visitors travel the furthest?

4 Which is nearer to Glasgow;
   a) Belfast or Aberdeen?
   b) Manchester or Hull?
   c) London or Bristol?

5 Describe the route by car to Glasgow from
   a) Plymouth   b) London
   c) Aberdeen   d) Newcastle

Main forms of transport used by visitors to Glasgow.

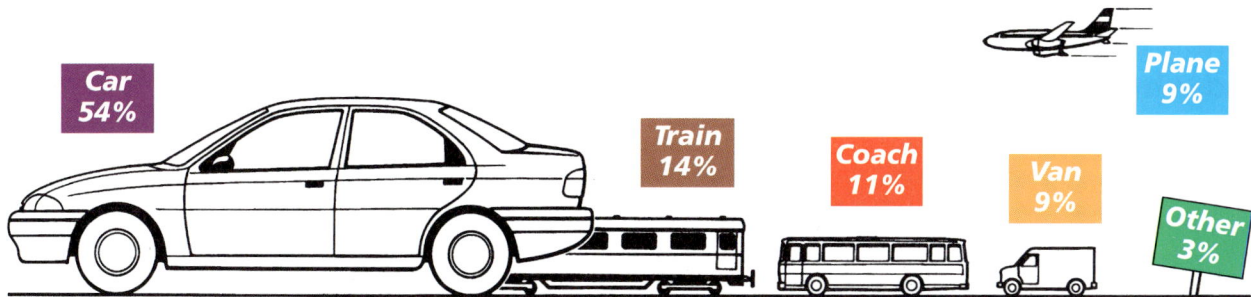

Car 54%

Train 14%

Coach 11%

Van 9%

Plane 9%

Other 3%

6 Which is the most popular form of transport?

7 Which is the most popular form of public transport?

8 Why do you think fewer people travel by plane than by train?

The picture shows the six most popular reasons why people visit Glasgow.

9 Describe each of the six most popular reasons why visitors come to Glasgow.

10 Which three are the most energetic?

11 Which costs the most?

12 List three you would like best. Say why?

The world comes to Glasgow

Why do large cities need foreign visitors?

Foreign visitors spend money on accommodation, food and drink, and in shops. This helps provide jobs in the hotel, restaurant and shopping industries. Visitors come to Glasgow as tourists or on business.

These charts show **where** foreign visitors come from to visit Glasgow and **when** they come.

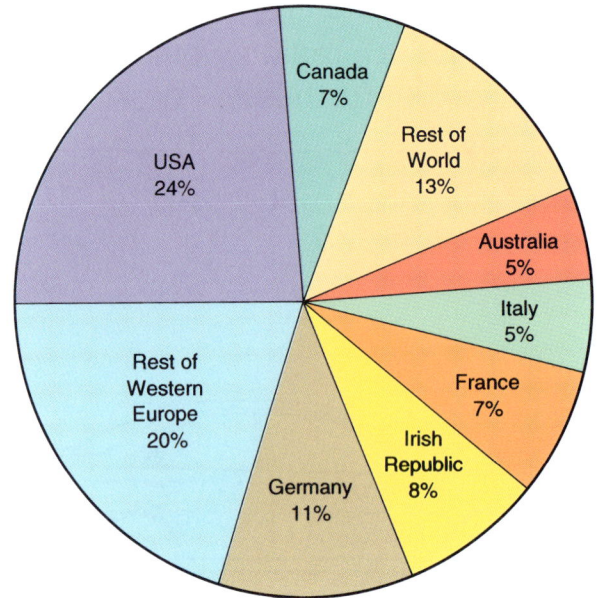

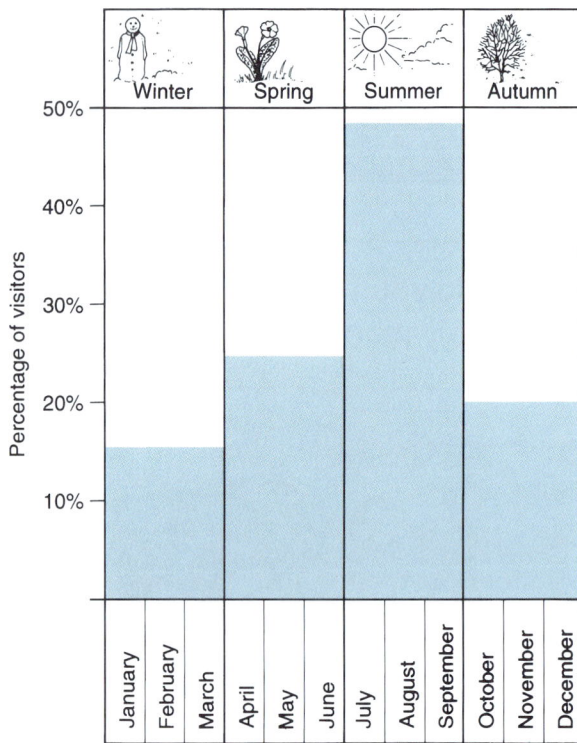

Pie chart: USA 24%, Canada 7%, Rest of World 13%, Australia 5%, Italy 5%, France 7%, Irish Republic 8%, Germany 11%, Rest of Western Europe 20%

Bar chart: Percentage of visitors by month — Winter, Spring, Summer, Autumn

Tasks

1 From which country do most visitors come?

2 From which continent do most visitors come?

3 From which countries do you think visitors are more likely to stay with relatives?

Visitors to the region

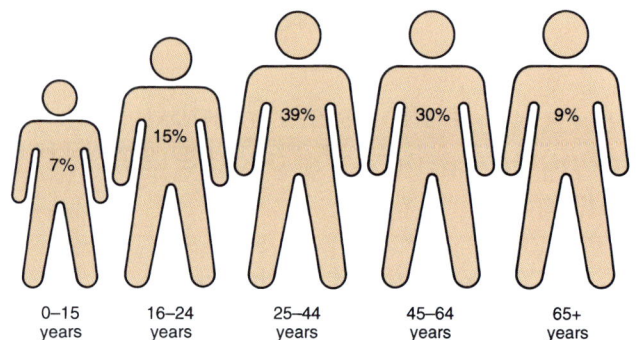

0–15 years 7%, 16–24 years 15%, 25–44 years 39%, 45–64 years 30%, 65+ years 9%

Tasks

4 Which season is the most popular? Why do you think this is so?

5 Which group is more likely to come all the year round, tourists or business people?

6 Which age group would spend the least money? Why?

7 Which two age groups would contain most business visitors?

Britain is an island. Visitors travel by plane, ship or through the Channel Tunnel.

The map shows where visitors entered Britain on their way to Glasgow before the Channel Tunnel was opened.

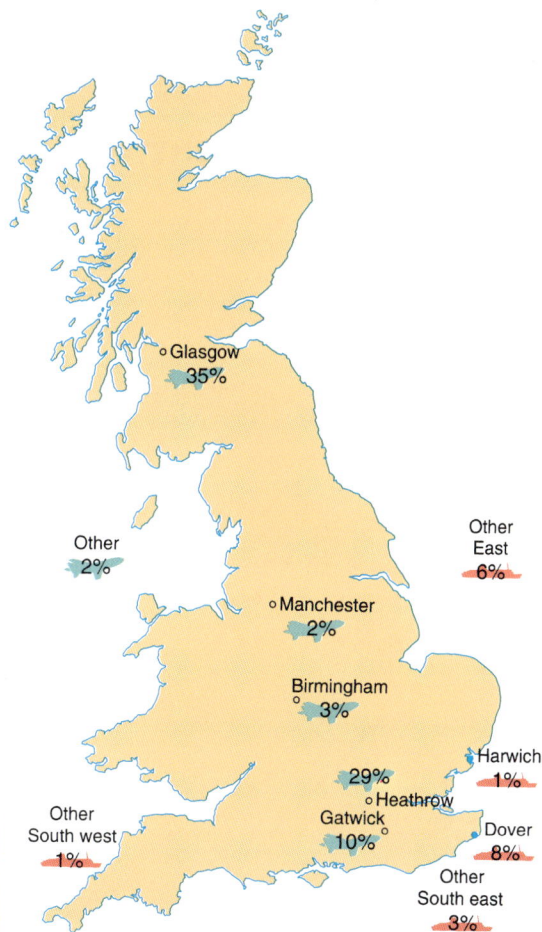

Tasks

8 Do most people travel by air or sea?

9 Which is the most popular port?

10 Which is the most popular airport?

11 Do most visitors to Glasgow arrive in Scotland or travel via England?

Glasgow
35%

Other
2%

Other East
6%

Manchester
2%

Birmingham
3%

Harwich
1%

29%
Heathrow
Gatwick
10%

Dover
8%

Other South west
1%

Other South east
3%

BAA
Glasgow International Airport

FAIRLINE SCOTLAND

54% of visitors stay in hotels or guest houses

30% stay with friends or relatives

9% stay in hostels or universities

12 What other type of accommodation could visitors use?

Tasks

13 Which of the three types listed above costs the most?

14 Which provides the most work for people in Glasgow?

Britain's weather

Is there a pattern to the weather?

Oban

°C | mm

Annual rainfall 1451mm

Edinburgh

°C | mm

Annual rainfall 642mm

Penzance

°C | mm

Annual rainfall 1131mm

London

°C | mm

Annual rainfall 599mm

Key

Land over 200m

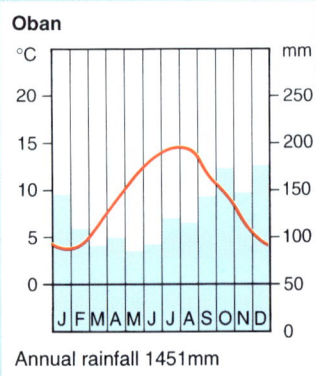

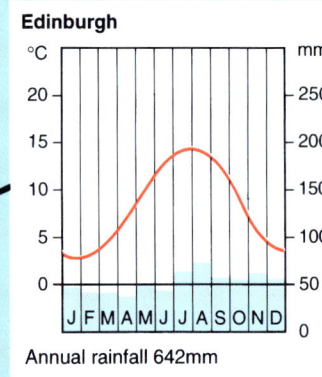

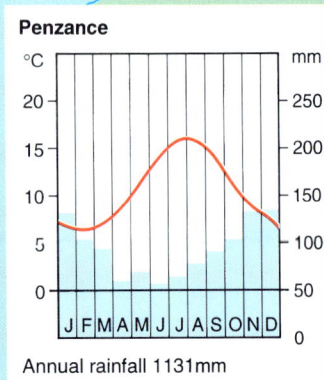

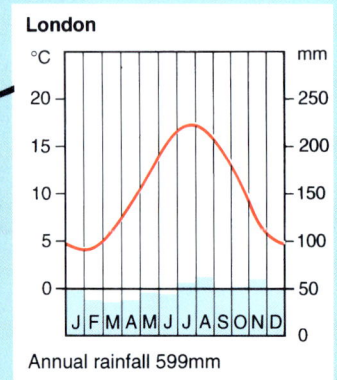

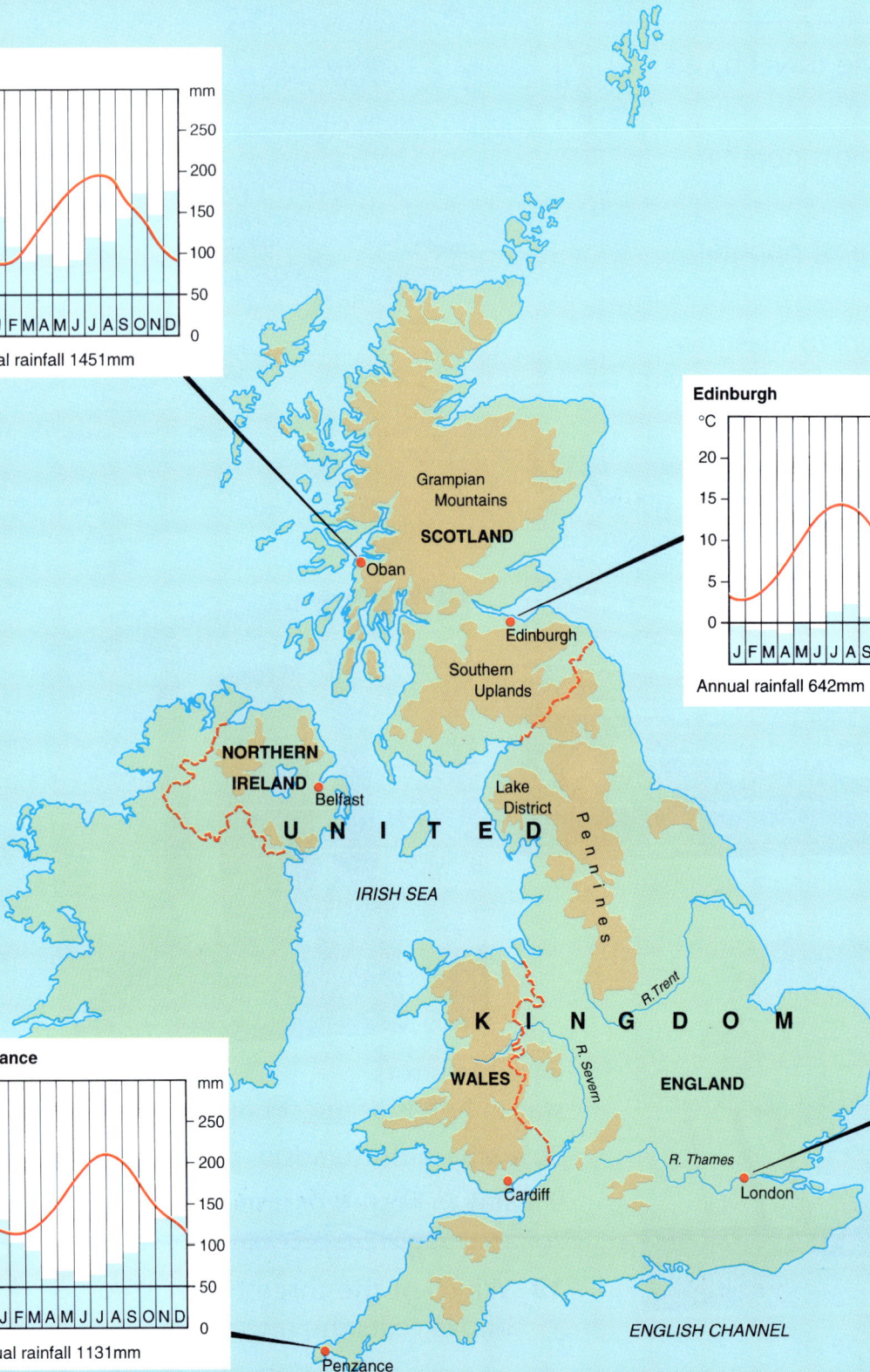

Grampian
Mountains

SCOTLAND

Oban

Edinburgh

Southern
Uplands

**NORTHERN
IRELAND**

Belfast

Lake
District

U N I T E D

Pennines

IRISH SEA

R. Trent

K I N G D O M

R. Severn

WALES

ENGLAND

Cardiff

R. Thames

London

0   100km

ENGLISH CHANNEL

Penzance

Look at the weather graphs on page 42.

1 List the annual rainfall for each place from wettest to driest.

2 Are the two driest places in the west or the east?

3 Copy and complete the chart.

Place	Months of the year			
	wettest	**driest**	**hottest**	**coldest**
London				
Edinburgh				
Penzance				
Oban				

Cold air from the Arctic travels over the Atlantic becoming warmer and very wet.

Air from northern Europe is very cold in winter but dry.

Warm air crosses the Atlantic from the south and is cooled. It brings warm, damp weather to the south-west.

Hot dry air from North Africa brings hot weather with little cloud in summer.

Britain is strongly affected by the westerly winds which move across the North Atlantic bringing windy, wet weather. The wettest parts of Britain are the high mountains in the west. Land east of the mountains is drier.

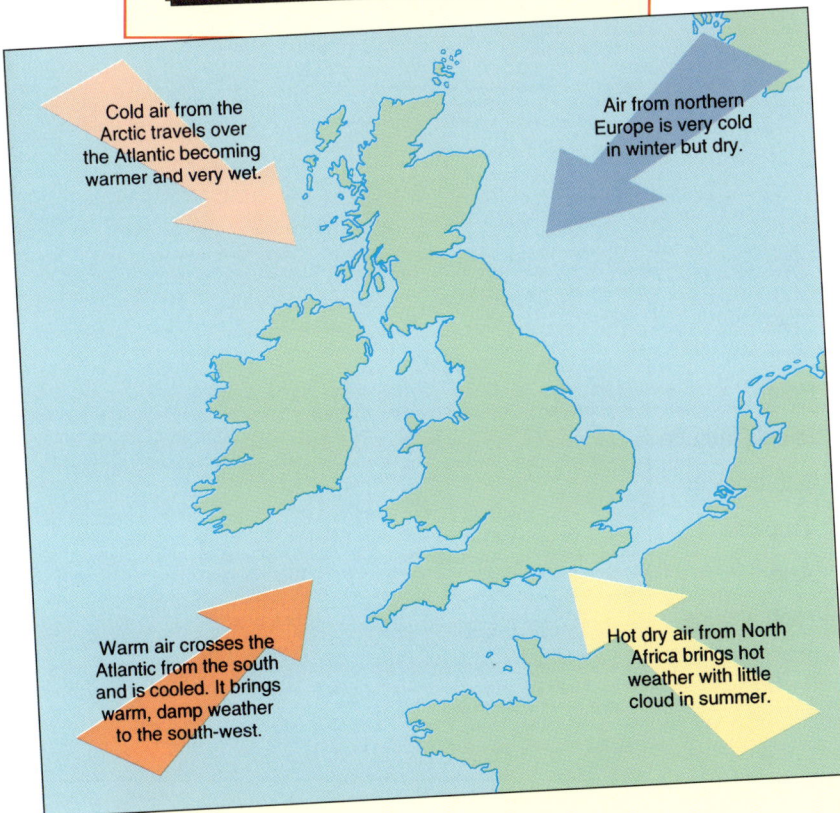

6 Which countries and seas might air from North Africa cross on its way to Britain?

7 Fill in the missing words

Winds from the _____ are usually wet.

Winds from the south are usually _____ .

4 Why do you think land to the east of the mountains is drier than in the west?

5 Why is air from the Arctic cold when it begins its journey?

43

LIVERPOOL HOPE UNIVERSITY COLLEGE

The map shows different types of climate around the world. The climate of a place is affected by:
- distance from the Equator
- distance from the coast
- height of the land
- wind strength and direction

The graphs are of five places with different climates.

Did you know?

Climate is patterns of weather based on records kept over a number of years.

Tasks

1 List the types of climate in Australia.

2 Which is the main climate type at the Equator?

3 Between which two lines are most of the world's deserts?

4 Which of the five climates shown in the graphs is nearest to that of London?

5 Copy and complete the chart. You will need an atlas.

Arctic Circle

2 Minneapolis

3 Pa

Tropic of Cancer

Equator

Tropic of Capricorn

- Polar
- Middle latitude
- Sub tropical
- Tropical
- Arid
- High altitude

Antarctic Circle

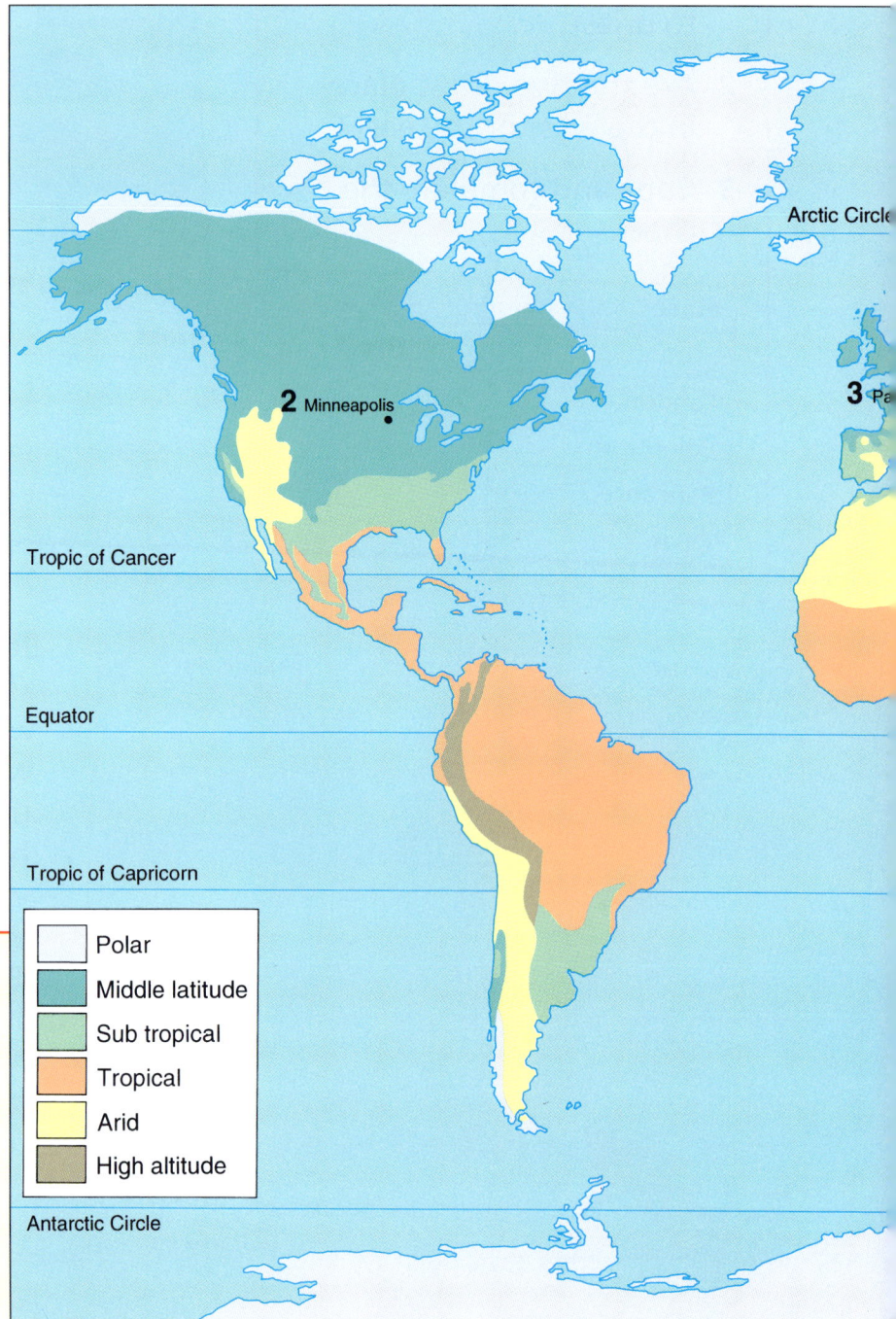

Place	Name	Country	Continent	Climate
1				
2				
3				
4				
5				

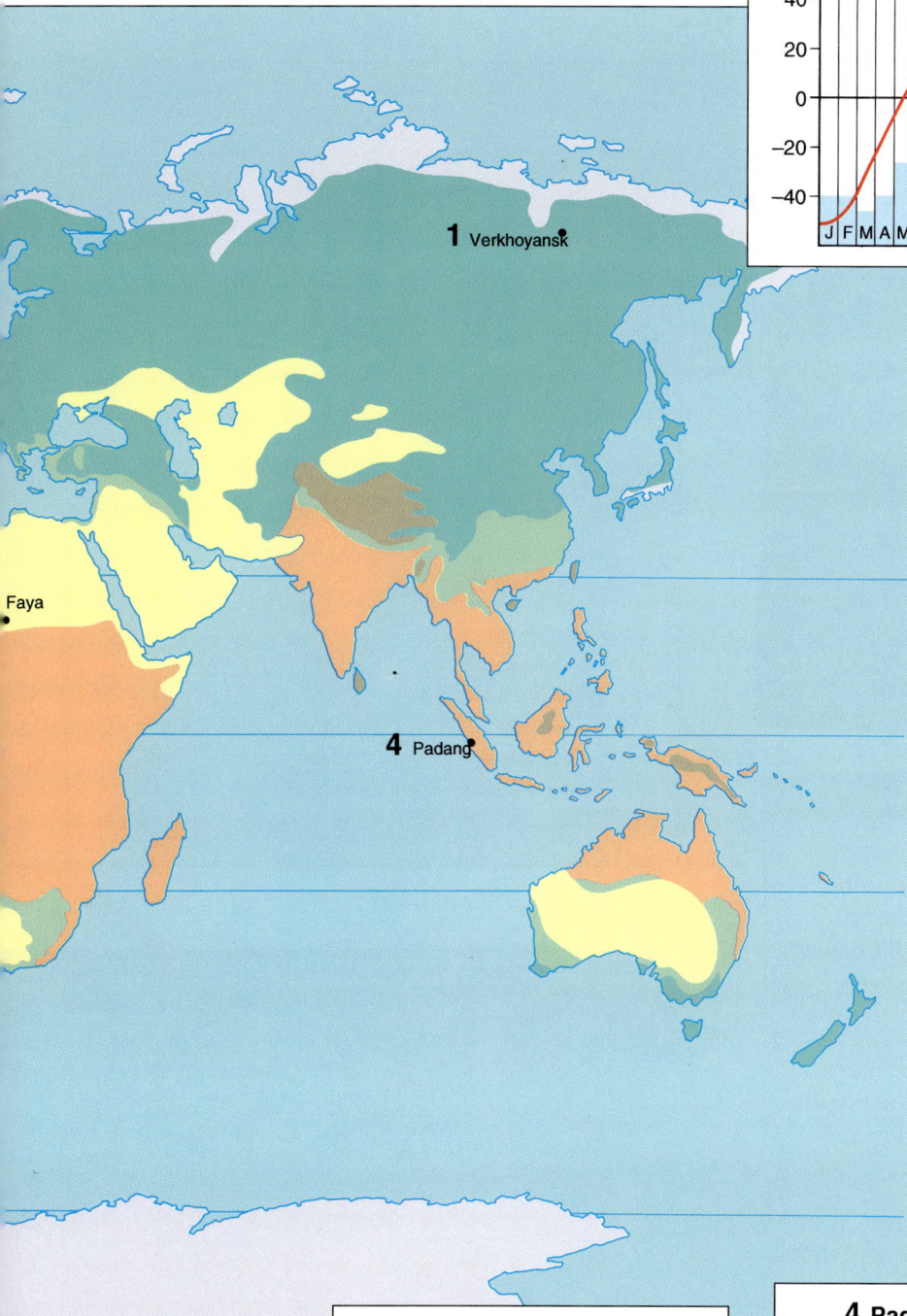

1 Verkhoyansk
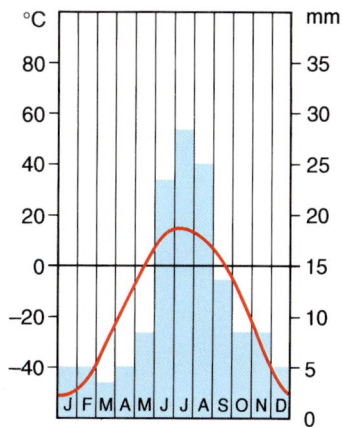

°C | | mm
80 | | 35
60 | | 30
40 | | 25
20 | | 20
0 | | 15
−20 | | 10
−40 | | 5
J F M A M J J A S O N D | | 0

2 Minneapolis
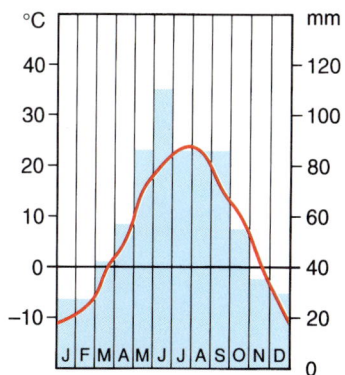

°C | | mm
40 | | 120
30 | | 100
20 | | 80
10 | | 60
0 | | 40
−10 | | 20
J F M A M J J A S O N D | | 0

3 Paris
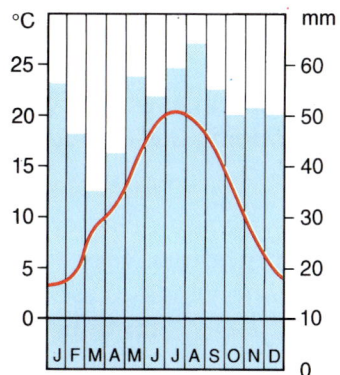

°C | | mm
25 | | 60
20 | | 50
15 | | 40
10 | | 30
5 | | 20
0 | | 10
J F M A M J J A S O N D | | 0

5 Faya
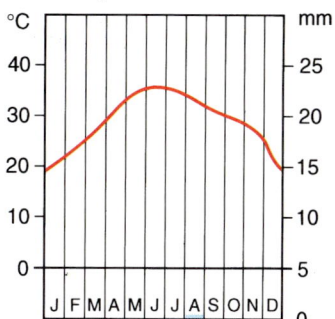

°C | | mm
40 | | 25
30 | | 20
20 | | 15
10 | | 10
0 | | 5
J F M A M J J A S O N D | | 0

4 Padang
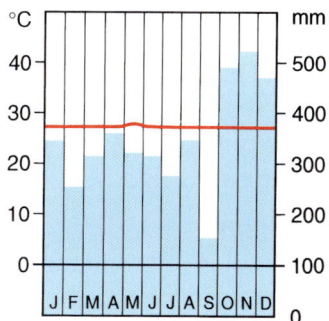

°C | | mm
40 | | 500
30 | | 400
20 | | 300
10 | | 200
0 | | 100
J F M A M J J A S O N D | | 0

45

Extremes

The climate in different parts of the world affects the type of landscape found there.

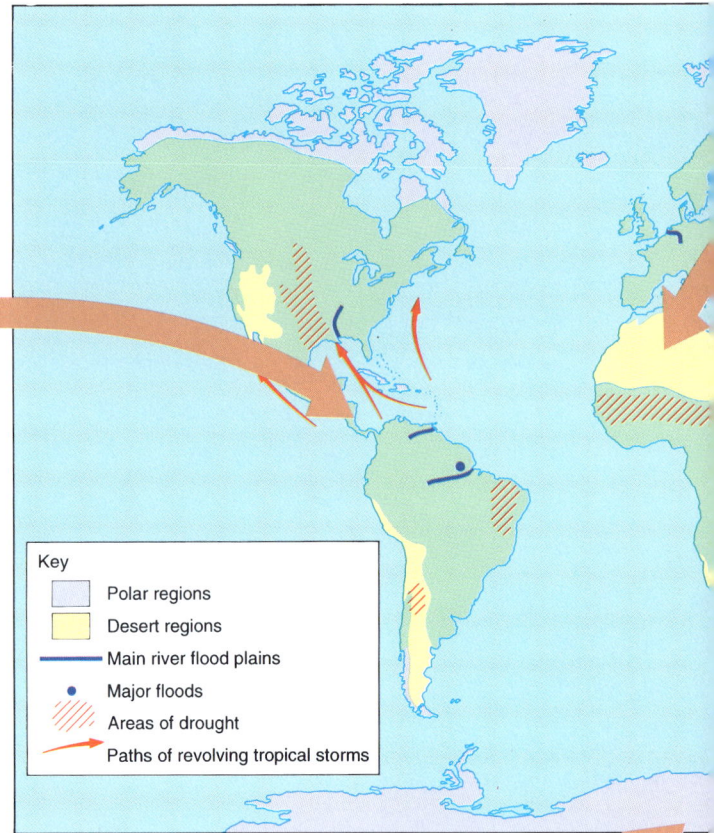

Key

- Polar regions
- Desert regions
- —— Main river flood plains
- • Major floods
- /// Areas of drought
- → Paths of revolving tropical storms

Did you know?

Monsoon
Monsoon is the rainy season when winds blow from the sea over the land carrying great volumes of rain. Monsoons can cause flooding but without them crops die.

Tropical storms
These are also called **cyclones**, **hurricanes**, and **typhoons**. They are storms which spin with winds up to 350kph, carrying torrential rain.

Deserts
Hot deserts are dry places where few plants or animals can survive. They do not receive winds which carry rain.

Polar
The Arctic and Antarctic are always cold. Even in summer the sun is too weak to provide warmth. The only people living in Antarctica are scientists.

Drought
In many regions rainfall is unpredictable. When drought occurs for a long time, the area can turn into desert.

47

Tasks

1 Are most areas of drought close to or far away from deserts?

2 Name three countries affected by hurricanes. Use an atlas.

3 Between which two lines do all hurricanes begin?

Complete the sentences

4 Hurricanes begin near the E_____

5 _____ is the only continent where no children live.

6 Monsoon winds do not blow over d_____.

7 Which continents have no hot deserts?

8 Which continents are not affected by hurricanes?

9 Copy and complete the chart.

Photo	Extreme	Advantage	Disadvantage
A			
B			
C			
D			
E			

How well do you know this book?

Copy and complete the crossword.

To find the answers you will need to look back through this book.
Use the contents page to help find the correct section.

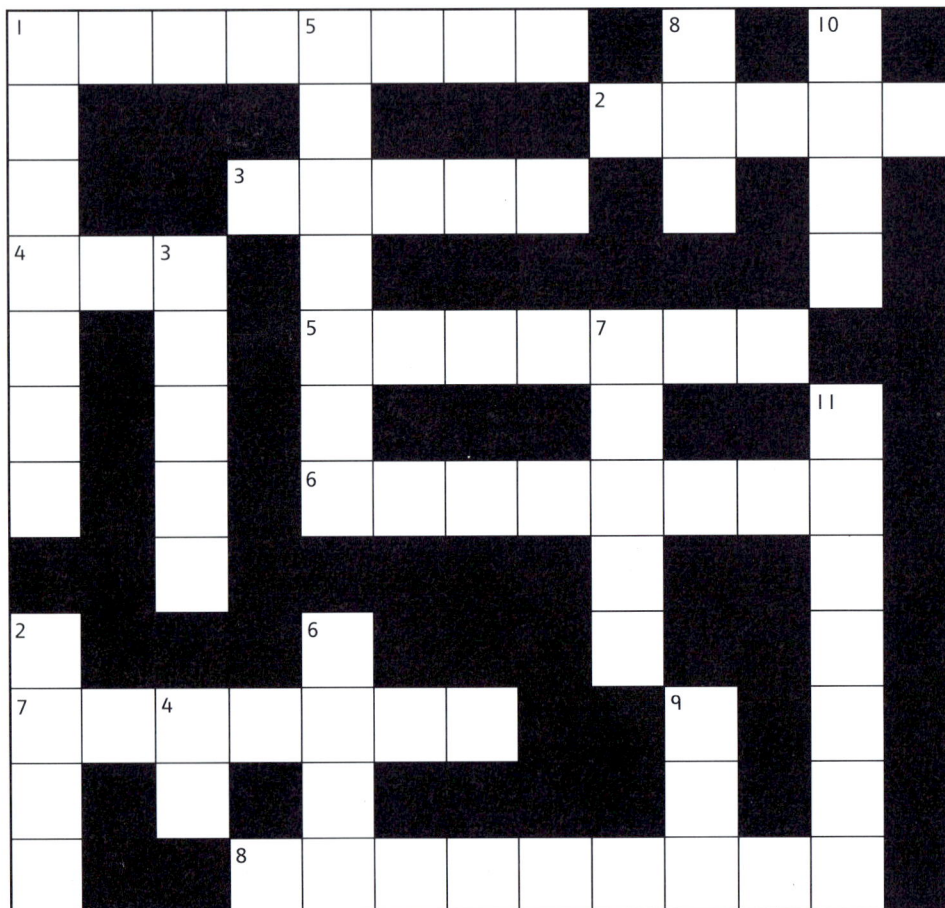

Across

1. River which passes through Barmouth (8)
2. Not urban (5)
3. Climate at the Poles (5)
4. Causes evaporation (3)
5. Scotland's largest city (7)
6. Climate in the Tropics (8)
7. Where a river meets the sea (7)
8. Service to transport the sick (9)

Down

1. Wet season (7)
2. Stream (4)
3. Compass direction (5)
4. Weather forecast appears here nightly (2)
5. No rain (7)
6. Plant which grows in hot climates (4)
7. Movement (5)
8. Seen in spring (3)
9. Rivers do this downhill (3)
10. Opposite of west (4)
11. Average weather (7)